592
DOR

Doris, Ellen.

Copy 2

Invertebrate
zoology.

$15.95

02286

DATE			

real kids
real science
BOOKS

Invertebrate Zoology

"Study nature, not books." —LOUIS AGASSIZ

Invertebrate Zoology

written by Ellen Doris
original photography by Len Rubenstein

PRODUCED IN ASSOCIATION WITH
The Children's School of Science
Woods Hole, Massachusetts

THAMES AND HUDSON

What is this book about?

Invertebrates, or animals without backbones, comprise about ninety-five percent of all animal life. This book focuses on seven phyla of invertebrates, most of which should be quite easy for you to collect and observe. You will find lots of projects, field trips, ideas, and suggestions for exploring the world of the invertebrates yourself.

How to use this book

Invertebrate Zoology is organized as a collection of separate experiments, investigations, and discoveries. It shows you where to look for insects, and how to study them once you find them. Though some basic terms and concepts are introduced in the first few sections, you don't have to follow the book step by step from beginning to end. We suggest you browse through it first. Look for a field trip that's easy to do near your home. Or you may want to go to your local fish store and get a clam or mussel to dissect as described on page 33. Also, this book will be a lot more fun if you share some of the projects and field trips with someone else, a friend or a parent.

Where can you get specimens and subjects to study? And equipment?

First of all, try to collect them yourself. And adapt equipment that you already have at home, like an old aquarium. But, you'll be surprised to find how many live samples and equipment can be ordered from biological supply houses at pretty reasonable costs. There is a list of equipment and specimens on page 62, but don't feel you have to order all of it at once. You'll be surprised at how much you can find and adapt yourself.

What is an imago? And how do you pronounce Platyhelminthes?

Check out the Glossary on page 63, which defines all terms that are printed in bold type. But don't get bogged down trying to pronounce long Latin names; sound them out as best as you can and go on.

Think for yourself

You'll probably have to adapt some of the projects you find in this book. You may not live near an ocean, a field, or a pond. But most big city parks have a wide range of insects and worms. Remember, not every project works according to plan. For instance, the crickets you are raising may not lay eggs, or the eggs they lay may not hatch. Think about why—are you sure you have a female? did you get the eggs too damp when you moistened the container?—and try again.

The Children's School of Science
Woods Hole, Massachusetts

Each summer, in an old-fashioned schoolhouse whose rooms are crowded with plants, nets, microscopes, and bubbling aquaria, several hundred children between the ages of seven and sixteen attend classes for two hours each morning. Led by teachers who are experts in their field, the children take frequent field trips and work with each other on projects and experiments. The classes are informal, and courses range from Seashore Exploration to Ornithology to Neurobiology. For over seventy-five years, this remarkable institution has fostered the joy of discovery by encouraging direct observation of natural phenomena.

Contents

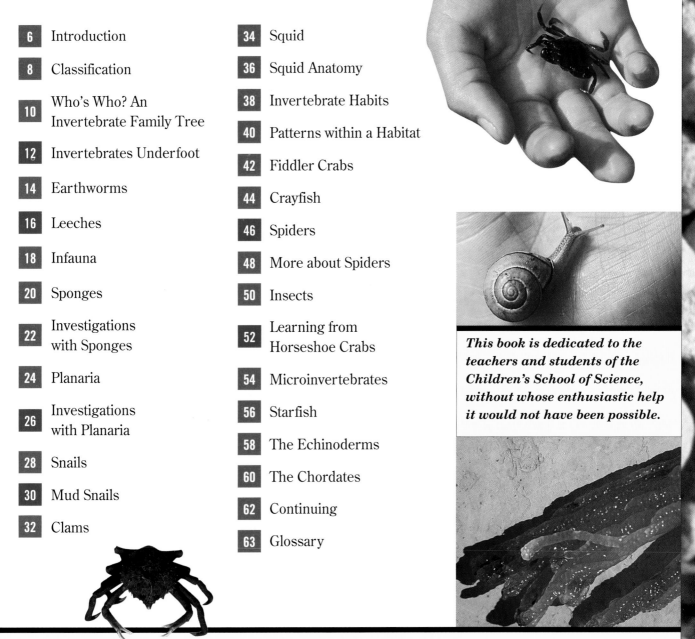

This book is dedicated to the teachers and students of the Children's School of Science, without whose enthusiastic help it would not have been possible.

Copyright © 1993 Thames and Hudson Inc., New York
First published in the United States in 1993 by Thames and Hudson Inc., 500 Fifth Avenue, New York, New York 10110

Photos copyright © Len Rubenstein unless otherwise indicated.

Library of Congress Catalog Card Number 92-62480

Designed, typeset, and produced by Beth Tondreau Design ■ Managing Editor, Jeanne-Marie Perry

Color separations made by The Sarabande Press ■ Printed and bound in Malaysia

Introduction

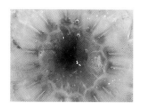

What do jellyfish, earth-worms, grasshoppers, and horseshoe crabs all have in common? Not much, yet they are all **invertebrates**, or animals without backbones.

Most animals are invertebrates. In fact, invertebrates make up about ninety-five percent of the animal species that have been discovered on Earth. The other five percent are the **vertebrates**, or animals that have a skeleton with a backbone. Codfish, rattlesnakes, ostriches, and people are all vertebrates.

Invertebrates and vertebrates— what these labels tell and don't tell

When scientists classify an animal, they usually group it with others that share important physical characteristics and evolved from the same ancestors. For instance, scientists group all birds together in one large class, Aves. The members of this class lay eggs, have feathers, and evolved from reptiles millions of years ago.

The invertebrates form a different kind of group, a group without a common ancestry or body structure. Knowing an animal is an invertebrate won't tell you to what other animals it is closely related. Starfish and leeches are both invertebrates, yet scientists think starfish are more closely related to people than to leeches. And, invertebrates often look dramatically different from one another. Lobsters, for example, have many pairs of legs and a hard covering on the outside of their bodies. Earthworms have soft bodies and no legs.

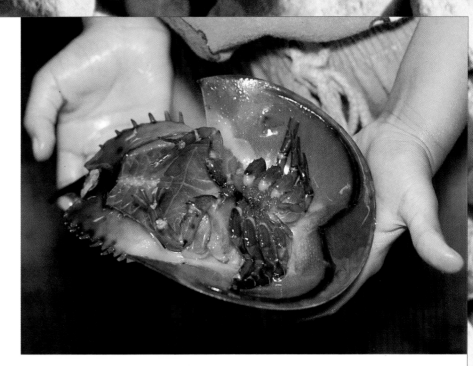

Vertebrates have backbones and invertebrates do not. Dividing up all the animals in the world into these two groups creates one enormous, diverse group and a much smaller, more **homogeneous** one. This man-made division reflects our interest in the animals that are most like us, and our tendency to lump together and have trouble distinguishing animals that are quite different than we are. Perhaps that's the best reason to study invertebrates—to learn to distinguish among this fascinating, vast, and varied group of animals.

Getting to know the invertebrates

Invertebrate zoology is such a broad field that scientists usually specialize in a particular aspect of it. Some focus on spiders or insects while others try to learn how various species behave, grow, fight disease, or affect neighboring organisms. This book will also specialize. Instead of describing thousands of animals, it will introduce you to a few that are easy to find and fun to study. As you get to know these animals, you will discover which aspects of invertebrate zoology most interest you.

Classification

o one really knows how many animals live on this planet. Well over a million different kinds, or **species**, have been described and named already. Scientists think there might be a million or two more that exist, but just haven't been discovered yet.

Millions of animals

It's hard to imagine one or two million different animals! How can we make sense of such diversity? One way is to categorize animals, or put them into groups, instead of thinking of an endless list of individual species. People often invent categories that express the important similarities and differences we see among animals. For instance, we speak of **domestic animals**—pets, livestock, and other animals we breed and raise—and **wild animals**—those that breed and find food without our intervention. And we speak of **pests**—those creatures that eat our food crops or damage our property—and **beneficial animals**—those that eat our pests or provide us with food or materials. Scientists have devised systems of classification that attempt to reflect what they understand about the evolutionary history of different animals, as well as their anatomy, physiology, and ecology.

Taxonomy

Scientists have divided up the million or so known animals into about twenty-six groups. (Scientists don't all agree about this division; some combine or further divide groups.) These groups are called **phyla**. Phyla are broad collections of animals that have important things in common, but may be quite different from one another in appearance and habit. For example, we belong to the phylum Chordata, as do guinea pigs, hummingbirds, herring, bullfrogs, sea squirts, lancelets, and lampreys. Tarantulas, butterflies, horseshoe crabs, shrimp, and pillbugs all share the phylum Arthropoda.

Phyla are divided into **classes**, classes into **orders**, orders into **families**, and families into **genera**. Each time a division is made, the animals that are most closely related are grouped together. Finally, animals are sorted into distinct species. Members of a species can reproduce to create more animals like themselves.

Scientists who are primarily interested in the classification of the animals they study are called **taxonomists**.

Phylum Chordata   *Phylum Arthropoda*

Naming animals

Many animals have more than one name, and many share a name with other species. "Grasshopper" and "locust" both name the same animal. Grasshopper and locust also name dozens of other, similar looking animals! To avoid confusion, scientists use a two-part Latin name to label each species. *Dissosteira carolina* names the Carolina grasshopper; the first part of the name is shared by all the related species that make up one genus, while the second part is given to just one species. Both common and scientific names will be used throughout this book.

Some invertebrates look so much alike that it takes an expert to identify each to the level of species. Often, you will be satisfied to simply know what phylum or class a particular animal belongs to. Taxonomy boxes will list this information for most of the animals pictured in this book.

Taxonomy

PHYLUM:
  Arthropoda (animals with paired, jointed legs and a hard exoskeleton)
CLASS: *Insecta (the insects)*
ORDER: *Orthoptera (crickets, grasshoppers, praying mantids, and their relatives)*
GENUS: *Dissosteira*
SPECIES: *Dissosteira carolina (carolina grasshopper)*

9

Who's Who?

ll twenty-six of the phyla that make up the animal kingdom contain invertebrates. Getting to know so many large groups takes time! Begin by learning more about the animals you already know a little bit about. Then move on to closely related species, or unfamiliar creatures that are easy to find, raise, and observe. This book will introduce seven phyla.

Characteristics of some invertebrate phyla

THE SEGMENTED WORMS—
phylum Annelida

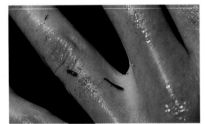

Leeches and earthworms are the most familiar annelids. All the members of this phyla have muscular, **segmented bodies** and simple brains. Annelid comes from the word *annulus*, which means "ringed."

THE SPONGES—
phylum Porifera
Sponges are a primitive group of **aquatic** animals with tiny pores covering the surface of  their bodies. They also have larger openings called **vents**. Sponges pull water in through their pores, extract food and oxygen from it, then push it out through their vents. *Porifera* means "having pores."

THE FLATWORMS—
phylum Platyhelminthes
The platy-helminthes are a large, diverse group of worms. Some are **parasites**, living in or on other animals, while others are **free-living**. Planaria, tapeworms, and flukes belong to this phyla. *Platy* means "flat" and *helminthes* means "worm."

THE MOLLUSCS—
phylum Mollusca

Clams, snails, octopods, and squid are all molluscs. Molluscs have a special body part called the **mantle**, which in many species secretes a material that hardens into a shell. *Mollusc* means "soft-bodied."

An Invertebrate Family Tree

THE ARTHROPODS—
phylum Arthropoda

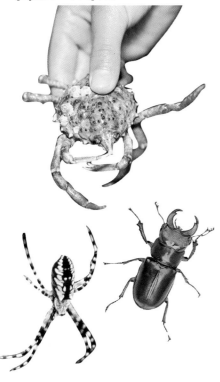

THE ECHINODERMS—
phylum Echinodermata

and **tube feet**. Starfish, sea urchins, and sand dollars are echinoderms. *Echinoderm* means "spiny skin."

THE CHORDATES—
phylum Chordata

Crabs, insects, and spiders belong to this group. Like other arthropods, they have paired, jointed appendages and an **exoskeleton** covering their bodies. Arthropods must **molt**, or shed their exoskeletons, in order to grow. *Arthropod* means "jointed legs."

Echinoderms are marine animals with bodies made up of five similar parts arranged around a central axis. Most have a hard internal skeleton

This group contains some invertebrate animals, like sea squirts and all of the vertebrates, including people. During some phase of their embryonic development or later life, all chordates have **gills,** a **dorsal nerve chord**, and a **notochord.** *Chordate* means "with a chord."

INVERTEBRATES

Start your search for invertebrates by looking on the ground. A yard or park is a good place to look. So is the edge of a pathway or sidewalk. You'll find insects, worms, and many other familiar invertebrate animals in these places.

Attracting invertebrates
Some animals are comfortable in dry air and bright sunshine. Others prefer cool, moist, shady places. Experiment to see what conditions attract different invertebrates by placing an old board or wooden shingle on the ground. You might want to label it so passersby know to leave it where they find it.

Check each day to see if any animals are under your shingle. Compare what you find under the shingle to what you find next to it.

Digging deeper
Japanese beetle larvae, earthworms, and centipedes are all invertebrates that spend a substantial amount of time underground. Avoiding fresh air and sunshine, they go about their business under our feet. Sometimes we get clues about life underground. Holes at the surface may lead to burrows and nests below. Soil-dwellers may search for food aboveground at night or early in the morning. Other times we have to search to discover what lives under us.

UNDERFOOT

Conducting a
soil-animal survey

A survey is a detailed study. To
find out what sort of animals live
underground, begin by surveying
a small area. You can work on
dry land, or in the wet sediment
along a pond shore or marsh.
First, mark off a square plot
measuring anywhere from six
inches to one yard on a side.
Then, gently remove the upper
few inches of soil with a garden
trowel and sift through it with
your fingers. Keep a record of
any animals you find. What do
they look like? How deep in the
soil did you find them? How
many of each kind were present?

Continue to remove and
search through layers of soil
until you've dug as deep as
you wish. Carefully replace
both soil and animals when
you are through.

Earthworms

 f you conduct a soil survey in a yard, garden, or woods, you'll probably uncover earthworms. These burrowing animals tunnel through the ground by pushing their "heads" through the soil and swallowing it in mouthfuls as they go. Swallowed soil is excreted and pressed against the walls of the tunnel, or carried up to the surface and deposited as **castings**.

Earthworms belong to the phylum Annelida. All annelids have segmented bodies that look as if they are made of many small sections.

What about them?

Earthworms have no eyes, but special light-sensitive cells in their skin allow them to tell light from dark. They usually avoid strong light, burrowing in the ground during the daytime and coming out to feed or mate at night. Earthworms are **hermaphrodites**; individuals have both male and female reproductive organs. When they mate, two pair up on the ground with their bodies alongside one another. Each transfers sperm to the other. A few

days later, each worm's "collar," or **clitellum**, starts to make a cocoon for the eggs. It slips like a band over the worm's body, picking up eggs and sperm as it does. Eventually, the cocoon slips right off the worm and into the soil. The tiny eggs within it hatch within a few weeks.

Raising earthworms

Housing: You can raise earthworms in a dishpan, picnic cooler, or gallon glass jar. Fill your container with loose, moist soil. Use soil that is high in organic matter rather than sand or clay. Try to gather soil from the spot where you collect your worms so you know that it will suit them. Keep the container away from direct sunlight, and mist the soil with water if it starts to dry out. Make a cardboard cover with holes for ventilation. A one gallon jar will house ten or twelve worms. Larger containers can hold many more.

Food: Earthworms eat fresh and decaying plants they find around their burrows, and organic matter found in the soil. Feed your worms every other week by sprinkling moist cornmeal or bread crumbs on top of the soil. You can also add a few leaves to the container. Remove uneaten food before it rots.

Habits: If you want to observe mating or feeding, you'll probably need to make observations at night. During the day, you can unearth a few worms and place them on damp paper toweling in order to get a closer look at them.

Buying worms: If you aren't able to collect worms outdoors, you can order them from one of the suppliers on page 62, or buy "nightcrawlers" sold for fish bait.

An earthworm experiment

Collect:

- two or three live, healthy earthworms
- a large, clean glass jar
- several soil samples of different colors (collect them from different depths or places)
- fresh leaves
- waxed paper
- a rubber band
- a paper bag or aluminum foil

Procedure:

- Layer the different soil samples in the jar. Mist the soil slightly if it is

extremely dry. Put fresh leaves on top of the soil and add the worms.

- Punch small holes in the waxed paper. Fasten it over the opening of the jar with a rubber band.
- Carefully observe the jar and record what you see.

- Place the jar in the paper bag and staple the bag shut. Keep it at room temperature for two weeks.
- Every few days remove the jar and study it carefully. How have the earthworms affected the soil?

15

Taxonomy

PHYLUM: *Annelida (the segmented worms)*
CLASS: *Oligochaeta (3100 species, including earthworms)*
ORDER: *Haplotaxida*
SUBORDER: *Lumbricina (includes three orders of earthworms)*
FAMILY: *Lumbricidae*
GENUS: *Lumbricus, Eisenia, and others (earthworms)*
SPECIES: *Lumbricus terrestris, and other species*

LEECHES

Bloodsuckers" is one name people have given leeches. But don't let their creepy nickname stop you from studying them. Leeches are fun to look for, interesting to watch, and easy to raise.

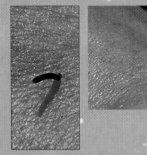  

16

Bloodsuckers and scavengers

There are many kinds of leeches, and each is attracted to a particular animal or group of animals. Some leeches prey on live snails, while others are scavengers and feed on dead fish. Still others parasitize turtles, live fish or frogs, and a few will even take blood from people. There are leeches that attach themselves to a host just long enough to get a meal of blood, and there are species that cling to a host most of their lives, leaving only to mate and lay eggs. Leech bites are painless, and leeches that are attracted to people aren't long term visitors; they drop off of their own accord as soon as they have finished feeding. If a leech gets on you, sprinkling a little salt on it will encourage it to drop off, full or not.

Collecting leeches

Like earthworms, leeches are annelids, and most are freshwater animals. Look for them in the shallows of lakes or ponds, and in marshes, streams, and brooks. You will sometimes see a large leech swimming gracefully through the water, but more often you will have to search for them. Many leeches are nocturnal and spend the day attached to the underside of stones, or buried in decaying vegetation or other debris that has settled to the bottom. Check common host animals, turtles or frogs for example, for clinging leeches. If you can't find leeches, you can order them from one of the supply companies listed on page 62.

Keeping leeches

Keep your leeches in a clean glass container with a tight-fitting lid with a screen top. Some leeches are active and will crawl right out of open containers. Leeches are sensitive to chemicals, like chlorine, that are sometimes added to tap water, so fill your container with spring or pond water instead. Change the water daily. Place a few stones on the bottom for the leeches to crawl under during the day, and store your containers out of direct sunlight.

Leeches don't need to eat often; one good meal goes a long way. Feed them weekly, or every couple of weeks. People who raise leeches often feed them just once a month, and some laboratory leeches have lived for two years without food! Some leeches will feed on bits of fresh liver, and others will eat live pond snails or earthworms. Watch how they feed. When a leech finds something to eat, it grabs hold of it with its suckers. Some leeches have a straw-like tube called a proboscis that comes out of the mouth to pull in food. Other leeches bite their hosts with three tiny jaws, then suck in blood. A chemical in their saliva called hirudin keeps the hosts' blood from clotting. A leech's stomach can hold a lot of food; some leeches may temporarily double, triple, or quadruple their weight during a feeding. Remove uneaten food after half an hour, clean the container, and add fresh water. If you can't find food that appeals to the leeches you have collected, observe them for a week or two, then return them to the place where you found them.

Take a closer look

Leeches have flat, segmented bodies with a disc-shaped sucker at each end that helps the leech move. The caudal sucker (at the rear end) and the oral sucker (at the front end) take turns gripping a surface while the leech pulls its body along, inchworm style. Some leeches are also good swimmers, and move through the water by wriggling their bodies.

Most leeches have eyes at the anterior, or front end, of their bodies. Some species have just one pair, but others have two, three, four, or even five pairs! The eyes aren't always apparent; look for them with a hand lens.

A leech life cycle

Like other annelids, leeches are hermaphrodites. When two leeches mate, each fertilizes the eggs of the other. Most newly hatched leeches are immediately independent and able to move and find food. But, it may be a long time before they are old enough to mate and lay eggs. Some leeches take as long as two to five years to mature. It is hard to know how long leeches live in the wild, but some laboratory specimens have lived a decade or more.

Taxonomy

PHYLUM: *Annelida*
    (the segmented worms)
CLASS: *Hirudinea (leeches)*
ORDERS: *Rhynchobdellida*
    and Arynchobdella

Infauna

ome animals live underground and underwater. Scientists refer to these aquatic burrowers as the **infauna**. Marine worms, clams, and many other invertebrates make up the infauna of a tidal marsh. At low tide, look for holes, castings, and other signs of animals living below the surface.

Trumpet worms

The trumpet worm, *Pectinaria gouldii*, lives in sandy estuaries as well as sediments further offshore. Also called an "ice cream cone worm," it inhabits a beautiful tube it makes from sand grains cemented together with **mucus**. The flattened head of the worm is at the wide end of the tube. On its head are golden

setae it uses for digging. An ice cream cone worm digs a U-shaped tunnel in the sand and buries itself upside down at one end. It pulls a current of water into the tunnel, past its head, and through the tube. This brings oxygen to the worm. Water is expelled through the rear end of the tube. The setae are also used to collect small particles of food from the floor of the tunnel, and to form a protective "door" to the tube when the worm pulls its whole body inside.

Shorebirds hunt for animals that live in the sand and mud.

Taxonomy

PHYLUM: Annelida (the segmented worms)
CLASS: Polychaeta (marine segmented worms, over 5000 species)
SUBCLASS: Sedentaria (polychaetes without teeth or jaws, among other characteristics)
FAMILY: Pectinariidae (worms that construct conical tubes. Golden setae used for digging and as an operculum, or door, to the tube.)
GENUS: Pectinaria
SPECIES: Pectinaria gouldii (ice cream cone worm)

Observing trumpet worms

A trumpet worm can be kept for a few days in a small glass bowl of **aerated** seawater.

Put a layer of sand on the bottom of the dish. You may get to see the worm add more sand grains onto its tube, or use its setae to dig in the sand.

Lugworms

Lugworm castings are a familiar sight in coastal areas with a mix of sand and mud on the bottom.

Lugworms stay in curved burrows, swallowing sediment and digesting the little bit of organic material it contains. The indigestible sand is excreted at the surface and forms a pile of castings. There are several species of lugworms in the genus *Arenicola*.

Both *Arenicola* and *Pectinaria* belong to the phylum Annelida, just as earthworms do. However, they belong to a different class called Polychaeta. Most marine polychaetes are **dioecious,** that is, both males and females exist.

Taxonomy

PHYLUM: *Annelida*
CLASS: *Polychaeta*
FAMILY: *Arenicolidae*
GENUS: *Arenicola*
  (lugworms)
SPECIES: *A. marina (common north of Cape Cod),
A. cristata (common south of Cape Cod),
A. brasiliensis (found on Cape Cod as well as in other parts of the world)*

The clam worm, Nerius viriens, *is another marine polychaete that you might find.*

Sponges

Mopping floors, wiping off tables, washing the dishes, washing ourselves: these are common chores we do every day. We are helped in our work by soap and water and sponges. Most of the sponges sold in stores today are machine-made of cellulose or foam. They are imitations of natural sponges, which are also sold for household use. We know what to do with sponges, but just what are they?

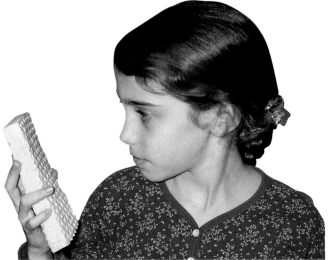

ART WERNEPER

Primitive animals

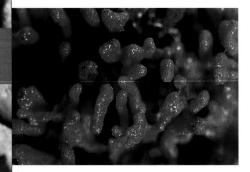

The natural sponges sold in stores were once living animals. It's hard to believe, since even when alive sponges don't move around, and they don't have any muscles or nerves. They don't have brains, mouths, stomachs, or hearts; in fact they have no organs at all! Not surprisingly, until about two hundred years ago, people thought that sponges were plants.

Today, scientists consider sponges the most primitive group of multicellular animals. They group all sponges together in the phylum Porifera. The lack of specialized tissues and organs is a striking characteristic of these animals.

Scientists have described about 10,000 species of sponges. Most live in the ocean, but there are some freshwater species, too.

The anatomy of a sponge

Sponges are usually irregular, or lumpy-looking, and full of tiny pores. In a living sponge, water is pulled through the pores into canals or chambers inside the sponge. Special cells with whiplike **flagella** move the water through these canals. They also filter bacteria, algae, or bits of decaying plant or animal tissue from the moving water. These tiny particles nourish the sponge. Filtered water leaves the sponge through larger holes or pores, called **oscula**.

Many sponges have a "skeleton" made of tiny, hard structures called

The holes that cover these shells are probably the work of sponges in the family Clionidae. These sponges live and grow in the holes they drill in old shells.

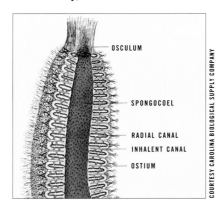

OSCULUM

SPONGOCOEL

RADIAL CANAL

INHALENT CANAL

OSTIUM

COURTESY CAROLINA BIOLOGICAL SUPPLY COMPANY

spicules. The spicules have sharp points like needles. Not many animals will eat sponges, and spicules are part of the reason why.

Finding sponges

Look for freshwater sponges on plant stems, stones, or pieces of wood you pull up from a pond or lake bottom. Freshwater sponges

are usually small and inconspicuous. Some marine sponges live in deep water and must be collected by a diver, or hooked up from a boat. However, you can find others in tide pools and on rocks or pilings in shallow water. If you are not able to find a sponge outdoors, you can order certain species from one of the supply companies on page 62.

21

Investigations with Sponges

Many sponges have spicules with a characteristic shape. When scientists are trying to identify a particular kind of sponge, they often take a close look at its spicules. To see spicules, you must **isolate** them, or separate them from the rest of the sponge, and put them under a microscope.

Isolating spicules

Take a small piece of living sponge and put it in a bowl with a little water and some chlorine bleach. The bleach will cause the sponge cells to turn pale and break down, and the clear, glass-like spicules will collect on the bottom of the bowl. Remove some spicules and place them on a glass microscope slide. What do they look like?

SAFETY NOTE: Chlorine bleach is irritating to eyes and skin, and it takes the color out of fabric, so use it carefully.

Regeneration

If a small piece of a sponge is cut or broken off, it can often continue growing. The broken piece simply becomes a new individual. This type of reproduction is known as **regeneration**. Commercial sponge growers depend on this ability. They take "cuttings" from a sponge, attach them to concrete blocks, and put the blocks in water. After a few years, the sponges have grown large enough to be harvested and sold. If you are planning to maintain a saltwater aquarium over a long period of time, you can try growing a new, whole sponge from a cutting.

Regeneration is just one way that sponges reproduce. They can also develop **buds** that break off and continue growing. Some species release bunches of cells called **gemmules** into the water. These gemmules eventually release cells that develop into adult sponges. Sponges can also produce sperm and egg cells that join together and grow into new sponges. Most individual sponges are hermaphrodites, capable of producing both eggs and sperm.

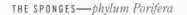

Reaggregation experiment

Damaged sponges can sometimes continue growing through a process called **reaggregation**. If you want to observe this, take a small piece of living sponge and squeeze it through a piece of nylon stocking. This will destroy the structure of the sponge, but not the individual cells. Collect the cells in a glass bowl filled with fresh seawater. Aerate the water and keep track of how the sponge cells look. As weeks go by, cells might reaggregate, or clump together and grow into a new sponge.

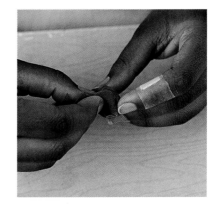

PLANARIA

Planaria belong to a large group of animals called the flatworms, or Platyhelminthes. Unlike annelid worms, their bodies are not segmented. Most flatworms are quite small. Many are parasites and live within the bodies of other animals, however, planaria are free-living. Planaria have smooth, flat bodies, and most species have just two eyes, though some have more. Their eyes simply tell light from dark, unlike ours which can form images and focus on near or far away objects. Most planaria avoid light, so scientists say they are photonegative.

Finding planaria

You can find planaria in streams, lakes, ponds, and other freshwater habitats. They are quite common, but you have to look closely to find them. Most are less than thirty millimeters long, and because they avoid light, they often spend the day under rocks or in decaying plants and bottom "muck." One good way to find planaria is to pick up a submerged stick or rock and turn it over. You may spot snails and leeches clinging to the surface, and tiny, brown or grey planaria gliding across. Even though they are small, the triangular heads and eyespots of planaria make them recognizable.

You can "fish" for planaria by tying a small piece of liver or other raw meat to a string and tossing it into the water. Half an hour later, pull the meat back up. Planaria that have come to feed on the meat will be pulled up along with it. This works better in running water than it does in stagnant water. Planaria get oxygen by absorbing it through their skin, or epidermis. In places where the water is stagnant and low in oxygen, you may have trouble finding them.

Planaria have been carefully studied in the laboratory, but scientists still have a lot to learn about the range and habits of different species in the wild.

Feeding

Planaria have mouths near the middle of their bodies, on the ventral (under) side. To eat, they stick a long tube called the pharynx out of their mouths. The pharynx works like a straw, sucking small particles and liquids into the stomach. Some planaria are particular about what they eat, and eject any unsuitable particles they ingest right back out through the pharynx. Planaria are sensitive to chemicals in the water. Special cells called chemoreceptors help them find food.

Reproduction

Planaria can reproduce by simply dividing and regenerating, or they can mate and lay eggs. Planaria, like all other flatworms, are hermaphrodites; each has both male and female sex organs. When two planaria mate, each transfers sperm to the other and both end up with fertilized eggs. Some species lay a number of eggs together in a capsule, or cocoon. The cocoons are attached to rocks and other objects by a small stalk. Eggs that are laid in the summer hatch in a couple of weeks. Those laid as winter approaches usually stay dormant until spring.

Commensalism

Some flatworms live on horseshoe crabs. Scientists consider these worms commensal, rather than parasitic, for though they live on the body of another animal, they do not seem to cause their host any harm.

Taxonomy

PHYLUM:
   *Platyhelminthes
   (the flatworms)*
CLASS: *Trematoda
   (parasitic flukes),
   Cestoda (parasitic
   tapeworms),
   Turbellaria (free-living
   flatworms, 3000 species
   described. There are
   some parasitic and commensal turbellarians.)*
ORDER: *Tricladida
   (includes freshwater
   planaria)*
FAMILY: *Planariidae*
GENUS: *Dugesia (most
   common laboratory
   planarian. There are
   a number of other
   genera of freshwater
   planaria as well.)*

Investigations with Planaria

Many kinds of planaria are easy to raise at home or in a lab. If you aren't able to collect wild planaria, you can order adults or eggs from a biological supply house (see p. 62).

Raising planaria at home

Put a few planaria in a clean container. A shallow glass baking pan or casserole dish will work, as will a stainless steel or enameled pan. Plastic containers are too hard to keep clean. Fill the container with bottled spring water, or water from the place where you found the

planaria. Don't use tap water; it may contain chemicals that are toxic to planaria. The water need not be deep; two inches is plenty. Add a few stones for the planaria to hide under.

Different species of planaria have different diets. In the wild, most eat tiny animals, and some feed on the bodies of animals that have recently died. Still others browse through the muck, eating whatever decaying plants and animals they find. At home, you can try feeding your planaria small pieces of liver or other raw meat. Some species will eat hard-boiled egg yolk. If these foods are rejected, you can try small worms or other live animals.

Give the planaria half an hour to feed, then remove leftover food. Rub your finger around the pan or dish to loosen any slime, and empty out the old, fouled water. Finish by filling the container with fresh water. Feed your planaria once a week.

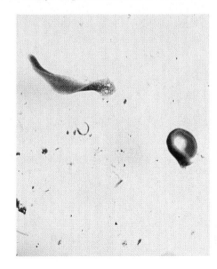

Regeneration

Most planaria can regenerate parts of their bodies. Growing back a missing part allows planaria to recover from injuries, and it's one way some species reproduce. This kind of reproduction is called **transverse fission**. It begins when a planarian's body starts to "pinch in" at the sides. A dividing line forms behind the pharynx. With its tail end holding onto the bottom, the head, or anterior end, of the planarian moves forward. Eventually, the two halves separate. Each regenerates the missing part, resulting in two half-old, half-new worms.

Regeneration has interested researchers who have discovered that if a planarian is deliberately cut in two across its middle, the tail end will grow a new head and the head end will grow a new tail. If one is divided lengthwise, the right half will grow a new left and vice-versa. To observe regeneration yourself, carefully cut a planarian in two with a single edged razor blade. Make note of where you make your cut, and make daily observations to see what changes occur. You will not need to feed regenerating planaria, but make sure to change their water every week.

Simple investigations

You can design simple experiments to find out more about planaria. For example, you can put them in a clear glass dish with dark paper under one half and light paper under the other. Do your planaria show a preference for one background over the other? You can also darken half of the container with a paper cover to see if they prefer light or dark areas. How do planaria respond to a current of water squirted out of an eye dropper? Do they respond differently when you direct a current at their heads than they do when you direct one at their sides or tail ends?

Research on flatworms

Barbara Boyer is doing research on the flatworm *Hoploplana*. She observes the way its eggs divide and develop into embryos, in order to better understand how the different ways that organisms develop have evolved. Scientists have noticed that some animals develop in similar ways. For example, if a cell is destroyed while an annelid, arthropod, or mollusc egg is dividing, the resulting embryo will lack the particular parts destined to grow from that cell. This is partly true of *Hoploplana*. Boyer has learned that it is not possible to predict exactly which structures will be missing when a particular cell is destroyed.

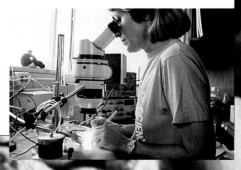

Snails

Snails belong to a group of soft-bodied animals that make up the phylum Mollusca. Many molluscs have shells. These shells are secreted by the mantle, a special body part unique to molluscs.

Land snails

Once in a while, a land snail shows up at the grocery store, accidentally shipped in with a load of produce. More often, you'll find them crawling around in the damp leaves on a forest floor, in gardens, or hiding out from the hot sun underneath a rock.

Land snails have four movable feelers, or **tentacles,** at the front end of their bodies. All of these are sensitive to touch, and the longer two have eyes at their tips. Land snails can tell light from dark, but their eyes don't form images.

How do snails move?

Snails are in the class Gastropoda, which means "stomach foot." A large, muscular foot runs the length of a snail's body. When the muscles in this foot contract, the snail glides along. Tiny hair-like **cilia** cover the bottom of the foot, and their movements also propel the snail. The foot, like the rest of the snail's body, is covered with slimy mucus.

The mucus lubricates, or greases, the surface the snail is on, helping it glide more easily. Watch a snail move along your arm or on the ground. You may see the shiny trail of mucus it leaves behind.

Eating

Most land and water snails have a special structure in their mouths called a **radula**. The radula is kind of like a tongue covered with rows of tiny teeth. A snail can use it to scrape away on food, filing off tiny bits and pulling them into its mouth. Some land snails have specialized diets, while others eat many different things. Many snails are **herbivores**, feeding on fruits, vegetables, leaves, and fungi. Some are **carnivores**, and eat worms and other snails.

Rearing land snails

You can keep one or two land snails in a gallon glass jar with paper toweling or coffee filters on the bottom. Use only white paper, as some inks and dyes may be harmful to snails.

A terrarium may seem like a more natural environment, but it's much harder to keep clean and mold-free. Make sure the jar has a lid so your snails don't escape. Wire screening or cheesecloth will let air in.

Remove the old paper and scrub the jar clean at least once a week. Thoroughly dampen fresh paper with water and layer it on the bottom. Moist paper will be easier for the snails to crawl on, and it will humidify the air. Humidity is

important. If the air and paper get too dry, your snails will **aestivate**, or pull their bodies into their shells and stick themselves to the side of the jar with mucus. This allows them to withstand unfavorable conditions, but it won't allow you to observe feeding and other interesting behavior. If the air is always very humid, or you don't clean the jar often enough, mold or bacteria might grow and kill the snails.

When you clean the jar, clean the snails off, too. Just rinse them in cool tap water. They are apt to come out of their shells and crawl around after their "shower," making this a fun time to hold and watch them.

Captive land snails will eat the damp paper you line the jar with,

so they are easy to feed. You can also give them a bit of lettuce, carrot, or apple on occasion. Make sure to remove leftovers and clean the jar after offering fresh food so that mold and bacteria don't grow. A small piece of oyster shell in the jar will provide the snail with a source

of calcium, a mineral needed for shell growth.

If you have to go away for a few weeks, your snails will probably not need any special care. Clean their jar before you leave, and add fresh, damp paper but no other food. As the paper dries out, the snails will aestivate. They can remain in this condition for a month or longer as long as the jar does not become moldy, freezing cold, or overheated. Keep the jar out of direct sunlight so the snails won't get overheated and die.

Taxonomy

PHYLUM: *Mollusca* (*soft-bodied marine animals*)

CLASS: *Gastropoda* (*snails, slugs, and limpets*)

SUBCLASS: *Pulmonata* (*slugs and most land snails. Mantle cavity has become a lung. Hermaphroditic.*)

ORDER: *Stylommatophora* (*two pairs of tentacles, with eyes on top of the second pair*)

MUD SNAILS

Snails don't just live on land; many are aquatic. Look for **marine gastropods**, such as *Nassarius obsoletus*, next time you visit the seashore. Commonly called the mud snail, or mud dog whelk, it lives along the east coast of the Atlantic Ocean and the west coast of the Pacific Ocean. It has a shell about an inch long, and lives in shallow, calm water with a muddy or sandy bottom. If you find such a place, go out near low tide to check for *Nassarius*.

A low tide scavenger

Mud snails bury themselves when the tide comes in. When it goes back out, they emerge, dirty-shelled, to look for food. Often hundreds crawl through the shallows and exposed mud flats. They are **scavengers**, feeding on dead crabs and fish, and small bits of organic matter they find in the sand.

Mud snails can't hear, and their two tiny eyes, located at the base of the two tentacles on their heads, are only able to distinguish light and shadow. Their soft body surface has special **tactile cells** that are sensitive to touch.

Observing feeding behavior

If you collect some mud snails and put them in a pan of seawater, you can watch them locate food and eat. Chemoreceptors on the tentacles and within the body detect chemicals in the water. They enable a mud snail to home in on a food source in the water, much as our noses allow us to follow a delicious scent wafting towards us through the air. Drop a piece of raw fish into the water and wait to see what the snails do. If they are hungry, you will see them turn and head directly for the fish. If they aren't hungry, they'll continue to rest or mill around with no apparent destination. You can remove the fish, wait a while, and try again.

Mud snails will head towards a piece of flesh, or even a chemical extract, from an oyster, crab, fish, or other marine animal. They won't, however, approach an injured member of their own species and eat it. Apparently, the smell of *Nassarius* meat repels rather than attracts them.

A mud snail has a long tube called a proboscis

that it extends in order to feed. Its mouth is at the end of the proboscis. Another tube, the siphon, pulls seawater into the snail's body and across its gill and osphradium, a chemically sensitive structure near the gill. By waving its siphon about, a mud snail can "smell" water drifting towards it from various directions, and choose a path that will lead it to food. Look for the proboscis and siphon when you watch a mud snail.

Taxonomy

PHYLUM: *Mollusca (soft-bodied marine animals)*

CLASS: *Gastropoda*

SUBCLASS: *Prosobranchia (mantle cavity is anterior. Aquatic sp. usually with one or two gills in mantle cavity. Shell, usually an operculum. Mostly dioecious.)*

ORDER: *Neogastropoda (marine snails, many are carnivorous. Have a proboscis with a radula with a row of three teeth. Oyster drills, whelks, olive and harp shells, among others.)*

FAMILY: *Nassariidae (dog whelks)*

GENUS: *Nassarius*

SPECIES: *Nassarius obsoletus (mud dog whelk)*

Clams

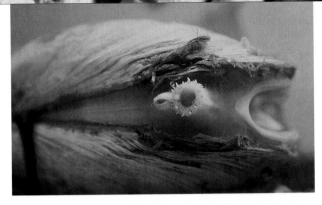

Clams spend most of their time buried in sand or mud. They use their strong, muscular foot to dig with. When you walk through the shallow water of a tidal flat or salt marsh, keep an eye out for siphon holes in the sand that tell you clams are below.

Clams, such as *Mercenaria mercenaria,* are **filter feeders**. Like many other aquatic animals, they eat the tiny plants, animals, and bits of decaying organic material suspended in the water. Unlike most other animals, they filter this food with their gills, the same organs they use to get oxygen out of the water. Clams eat to breathe, and breathe to eat. They can also get oxygen through their mantle, a layer of tissue just underneath the shell.

Water is pulled into a clam's body through the **inhalent siphon**, the one with a fringed end. The fringe helps keep sand and other debris out. After water is filtered, it is pumped back out through the **exhalent siphon**.

How old are you?

Mercenaria mercenaria starts out as a tiny, swimming larva, but as its shell and body grow, it buries itself in the sand. New shell is secreted by the mantle. As the clam gets larger, each **valve**, or half of its shell, grows around the edge. You can see lines that mark each season's growth, like the rings on a tree stump. You'll also notice a bump on each valve near its hinge. This bump, called the **umbo**, is the oldest part of the shell. By comparing the size of the umbo to the size of the entire shell,

Surf shell

Soft shell

you can see how much the clam has grown. You can also try estimating the age of a clam by counting its growth rings. Hard-shell clams like *Mercenaria* sometimes live twenty years or more!

Reproduction

Most clam species are dioecious; some are males and others female. Adults reproduce by pumping sperm or eggs out through their siphons. The eggs are fertilized in the water, then hatch into larvae. Some species, like the tiny "fingernail clams" you find in ponds, actually **brood** their eggs. The females keep their eggs inside their shells, on their gills. When males release sperm into the water, the females pull it in through their siphons. The fertilized eggs remain inside the female's shell until they hatch.

Dissecting a clam

Clams belong to the class Bivalvia, consisting of molluscs with a two-part shell. Mussels and oysters are also Bivalvia molluscs.

You can learn about the anatomy of **bivalve** molluscs by dissecting a clam. Buy one from a grocery store or fish market, or order a preserved specimen from one of the supply companies on page 62. A live clam will often close its shell tightly when removed from water. Freezing or boiling the clam will kill it and open its shell. Preserved specimens have to be opened by sliding a scalpel between the valves, and cutting through the two large muscles that clamp them together.

Inside you will see the large foot and the muscles that open and close the valves. You can also look for the gills, stomach, mantle, and **gonads**.

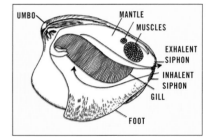

Taxonomy

PHYLUM: Mollusca *(soft-bodied marine animals)*

CLASS: Bivalvia *(molluscs with a two-part shell: clams, oysters, and mussels. Gills usually used for collecting food and getting oxygen.)*

SUBCLASS: Lamellibranchia

ORDER: Heterodonta *(fresh and saltwater clams, siphons usually present, a few large hinge teeth.)*

FAMILY: Veneridae

GENUS: Mercenaria *(common, edible marine clams)*

**SPECIES: Mercenaria mercenaria (quahog, or hard-shell clam)*

33

Once you have separated the valves, a clam's internal organs are easy to see.

Mya arenaria, *the steamer clam, cannot pull its siphons into its shell like many other clams can.*

Squid

Squid live in salt water. They eat fish, shrimp, and other marine animals. When a squid spots a school of fish, it darts in and grabs one. Its two long tentacles and eight shorter arms are lined with round discs like suction cups that keep prey from getting away. The squid uses its arms to hold the fish near its mouth, then bites off chunks with its beak. Squid prey on whatever crustaceans and fish they can catch. In turn, they are eaten by many kinds of fish, as well as whales, humans, and other squid.

The squid belongs to the class Cephalopoda, along with the octopus, cuttlefish, and nautilus. Cephalopods are molluscs, just as snails and clams are. Unlike most other molluscs, squid don't have external shells. Their mantles are easily seen on the outside of their bodies.

Squid come in many sizes. The smallest species are less than an inch long, while members of the genus *Architeuthis* may reach lengths of sixty feet. These giant squid are the largest living invertebrates. They are sometimes seen at the surface, but usually stay in deep water. They are fed upon by sperm whales.

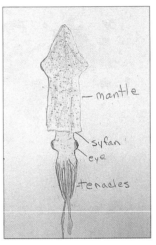

Depending on the species, squid can measure anywhere from less than an inch to sixty feet in length.

Going places

Squid move by jet propulsion. When water is taken in under the mantle and pushed out through a siphon under a squid's head, the squid moves backward. Squid can pump water gently and travel along at "cruising" speed, or suddenly expand and close the mantle, shooting quickly away from danger. The siphon can be "aimed," allowing a squid to change direction without turning its body around. Squid can even propel themselves right out of the water, and splash down as far as a hundred feet away, or land on the deck of a passing boat.

34

Changing color

Squid can change color. The dark spots on the head and mantle of a squid are **chromatophores**, special cells full of pigment. When tiny muscles around the chromatophores contract, these cells spread out like a flat plate, and the pigment they contain shows as colored splotches on the squid's skin. When the muscles relax, the chromatophores return to a more rounded shape, leaving just tiny dots of pigment visible. Squid often change color when they are disturbed. They can also use color to help attract mates, blend in with their surroundings, or escape predators.

Many species of squid make their own light, as fireflies do. Special light-emitting cells called **photophores** contain chemicals that glow when they react to something. Scientists aren't sure of the function of these lights; perhaps they attract mates or prey, or help schools of squid stay together. Squid are fast moving, reactive animals that are difficult to keep in captivity, so many aspects of their lives remain a mystery.

A Mop of Eggs

This strange object is a **mop** of squid eggs. It was started by one female who produced a number of strands and fastened them together. Other females came and added more strands. The result is this collection of eggs. Each finger-like strand of the mop contains about a hundred eggs. In about ten days, thousands of tiny squid will hatch.

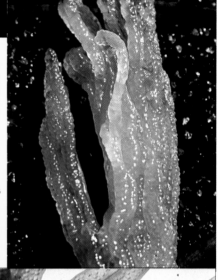

A squid's siphon, found underneath its head, helps propel and direct the squid through the water.

Taxonomy

PHYLUM: Mollusca
(includes soft-bodied marine animals)

CLASS: Cephalopoda
(includes squid, octopods, cuttlefish, nautili)

ORDER: Decapoda (cuttlefish and squid; lateral fins on body, 2 tentacles, 8 arms)

SUBORDER: Teuthoidea (squid and those decapods with a shell that is a flattened plate or pen)

GENUS: Loligo

SPECIES: Loligo pealei (Atlantic longfin squid)

35

Squid Anatomy

I f you live near the coast, you may be able to get a whole squid from a fish or bait store, or from a fisherman. Study its external body features, then dissect it to learn more about its internal anatomy.

External anatomy

Look closely at your squid to find the mantle, siphon, chromato-phores, and the suction cups on the arms and tentacles. The **mantle cavity** is the space underneath the mantle that fills with water during the first phase of jet propulsion. When a squid closes the edge of the mantle tightly around its head, water trapped in the mantle cavity squirts out of the siphon. Also look for the fins that stabilize a squid's body as it moves through the water.

Squid have many external body features that are easy and fun to find.

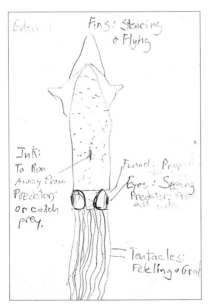

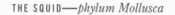

More squid studies

Squid have large eyes that help them find prey and avoid danger. Squid eyes are, in many ways, quite similar to our own. Each squid eye has an eyelid, lens, cornea, and retina. Dissection will reveal some of these structures. Squid have brains, and a highly developed nervous system that enables them to react extremely quickly when threatened. These characteristics have intrigued scientists who have made squid the center of their research. Many species of squid have giant nerve fibers a hundred times larger than our own. The size of these fibers makes them easier to study than the smaller fibers of other animals. Much of our current understanding of vision and the human nervous system derives from studies of squid.

Internal anatomy

You'll need a small, sharp pair of scissors to study the internal anatomy of a squid. Dissecting kits available from the supply houses on page 62 contain scissors. A dissecting pan filled with hard wax you can stick pins and probes into is useful but not necessary. A slab of styrofoam, a piece of thick, corrugated cardboard, or a soft pine board makes an inexpensive substitute.

Carefully cut through the mantle to find internal organs like the stomach and **ink sac**. You may be able to tell what a squid has been eating by dissecting the stomach and examining its contents. A long, stiff structure called the **pen** supports the body. Scientists think that squid may have evolved from molluscs with external shells, but over the years most of the shell disappeared. The part that remained became enclosed by the mantle and is now called the pen.

The old ink trick

Squid are famous for a remarkable ability; their bodies produce "ink" that squirts out when they are disturbed. The ink forms a dark cloud in the water, roughly the same size and shape as the squid that created it. Attacking predators are distracted by this inky imitation, while the real squid literally turns pale and jets away.

Invertebrate Habits

The seashore is a good place to find invertebrates from many different phyla, and to study the differences between species. Animals that live quite near one another may have different ways of coping with the same environment. How do coastal invertebrates settle down and make a living?

Slipper snails

Slipper shell, decker, boat snail, and slipper snail are all common names for the marine gastropod *Crepidula fornicata*. Its shell has a shelf across one end of the opening, and when empty, it reminds some people of a bedroom slipper or a small boat.

Slipper snails begin life as tiny **veliger larvae**. They swim through the water, filtering out small particles of food. Eventually, they settle down on some suitable object, metamorphose, and become adults. Just about anything firm enough for a slipper snail to hold on to makes an acceptable home. You will find them on rocks, old clam shells, live horseshoe crabs, and man-made litter. Once settled, they tend to stay put.

Reproduction

Often you will find slipper shells piled one on top of another. These groups contain individuals of both sexes and varying age. Oddly, a slipper snail's sex is linked to its age; all young *Crepidula* are males. After a while, the reproductive organs of these young males deteriorate. A period of transition begins where some males change into females, while others redevelop male reproductive organs. The sex of nearby slipper snails can influence one in transition. If females are scarce in a particular area, young males are likely to become females. But a male that enters transition attached to a female might well emerge a male. Once a slipper snail becomes a female, she will remain one for the rest of her life. A male slipper snail can mate if it is directly attached to a female. With part of its shell **margin**, or edge, touching the female, the male's penis can reach the female's **gonopore**, delivering sperm to her eggs. The female releases her fertilized eggs into the water where they hatch into another generation of veliger larvae.

Barnacles

You can find acorn barnacles attached to rocks, pilings, and seashells along the coast. They are **sessile** animals; they live in one place instead of moving around. Many animals can move to escape predators and harsh environmental conditions, or to locate mates and food. Sessile animals must accomplish all this while permanently "parked."

Starting out, settling down

Like many marine animals, an acorn barnacle starts out as a small, free-swimming larva. It has antennae, six pairs of jointed legs, and a **carapace**, or shell, covering its body. After several molts, it is ready to leave its free-swimming life and settle down. It attaches itself to a rock, shell, or other suitable surface with cement produced by glands near the antennae. This cement is extremely strong, and will keep the barnacle glued in place, even when heavy seas pound against it. Once cemented, the barnacle is attached for life. A series of hard plates grows around the carapace. Eventually, the barnacle looks like a small, greyish-white volcano. Two central pairs of plates, called the **scuta** and **terga**, form a "door" that can open and close.

As food goes by

Sessile animals can't roam around in search of a meal. Instead, they have to grab food as it goes by. Ocean water is full of single-celled algae and bacteria, microscopic animals, and bits of decaying organic matter. Barnacles collect this food by sticking their legs, or **cirri**, in and out through the open central plates. The cirri filter particles from the water, pulling them down inside the plates and into the barnacle's mouth.

Barnacles that live in the intertidal zone can only eat when the tide is high enough to cover them with water. At low tide, the door formed by the scuta and terga closes to protect them from drying wind and sun.

Reproduction

Often, many barnacles are crowded together on the same rock or piling. This makes finding and reaching a mate easy. One barnacle can extend its penis to fertilize the eggs of another cemented near it. Most acorn barnacles produce both eggs and sperm. A barnacle that settles down far from others of its kind can fertilize its own eggs.

The eggs develop and hatch inside the mantle wall of the parent, and the tiny larvae are released to begin life on their own.

Unlikely crustaceans

Barnacles remind many people of seashells, and they were once grouped with the molluscs. But a close look at their larvae, or at the adults inside their "shells," shows that they have paired, jointed legs and exoskeletons that they must molt in order to grow. Scientists now classify barnacles with the crustaceans, an arthropod class that includes lobsters, crabs, and shrimp.

There are about 900 different species of barnacles living in the ocean or along the shore. Many attach themselves to rocks, buoys, and other hard objects. Some live on other animals.

Taxonomy

PHYLUM: Arthropoda *(animals with paired, jointed legs and a hard exoskeleton)*
CLASS: Crustacea *(includes lobsters, shrimp, crabs, barnacles, and others)*
SUBCLASS: Cirripedia *(parasitic and free-living barnacles, some 900 species)*
ORDER: Thoracica *(free-living and commensal barnacles with six pairs of cirri. Mantle usually covered with hard plates.)*
SUBORDER: Balanomorpha *(sessile barnacles with mantle wall topped by paired, movable scuta and terga)*
GENERA: Balanus, Chthamalus, *and others*
SPECIES: Balanus balanoides *(northern rock barnacle),* **Balanus nubilis** *(giant acorn barnacle),* **Chthamalus fragilis** *(little grey barnacle), and many others*

Patterns within a Habitat:

Most invertebrates are adapted for life in a particular **habitat**. But within a single habitat, conditions vary from place to place. Seemingly minor differences can cause an animal to find one spot livable, and another quite near it completely unsuitable. When you go looking for invertebrates, take note of where you find each one. You may discover that a particular species lives on or near a certain kind of plant, or that two different invertebrates are often found in close association with one another. Scientists are interested in these patterns.

Observing along a transect

You can set up a **transect** on a beach, in a field, or in your yard in order to find out more about invertebrate patterns in a particular area. Observing along a transect is like looking at a cross section of an area.

To begin, find a **transect site.** Choose one at random by closing your eyes, throwing an object, and locating the transect where it lands, or select a particular site that interests you. Set up a **benchmark** by driving a stake into the ground, or marking a rock with paint.

Run a length of clothesline marked off in yards through your benchmark. You now have a transect line running across your study site. With the benchmark as your "zero point," you can easily refer to other points along the transect. Positive numbers are used to label each yard marked on one side of the benchmark, and negative numbers are used on the other.

To develop a sense of where different invertebrates live, place a wooden frame or plastic hula hoop

along the transect at various points. At each point, record the number and kind of animals you find within the frame. You can also record information about the physical environment, such as the temperature, water depth, or size of soil particles. Decide if you want to include soil animals in your study, or just those on the surface. If you are working at the shore, you can extend your transect out into the water and find out what invertebrates inhabit the shallows.

Who Lives Where?

Measuring elevation

When you set up a transect on a beach or hillside, you can use a level and two yardsticks to figure out how much the ground slopes. Begin by holding one yardstick upright at the benchmark, and another at "+1." Stretch the transect line taut between the two sticks, and check to see that it is level. Read each yardstick where the transect line crosses it. Subtract the reading on the "+1" stick from that of the benchmark stick to determine the difference in elevation between the two. You will get a positive number when there is an **incline,** or uphill slope, and a negative number when there is a **decline,** or downhill slope. Move your yardsticks to the "+1" and "+2" positions, and continue until you have measured elevation along the entire length of the transect.

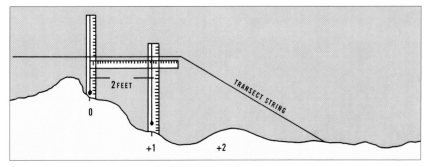

2 FEET

0   +1   +2

TRANSECT STRING

Using transect observations

Observing along a transect can help you learn about environmental variation and species distribution within a particular habitat. It can also help you compare different habitats.

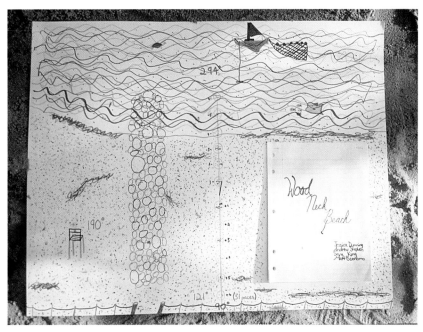

Fiddler Crabs

 Fiddler crabs are the small, burrowing crabs that make up the genus *Uca*. Some live in mangrove swamps, while others inhabit mud flats and salt marshes. Fiddler crabs can tunnel a foot or more into the ground, rolling up little balls of sand and carrying them to the surface with their legs.

When the tide is low, fiddler crabs crawl out of their burrows to look for food. They scoop small amounts of sand into their mouthparts, sift through it for bacteria and other organic matter, and "spit" out little pellets of indigestible sand. Fiddler crabs also eat decaying plants, and sometimes they eat each other. If you discover a burrow, look to see what size pellets are piled up at the entrance. Small ones tell you a fiddler has been feeding. Larger sand balls mean it's been digging. As high tide nears, fiddler crabs retreat into their burrows, plugging up the entrances with sand or mud.

Classifying fiddlers

Fiddler crabs belong to an enormous group of animals called arthropods. Animals in the phylum Arthropoda have jointed legs (or, if you translate "arthropod" literally, jointed feet). They also have a hard exoskeleton covering their bodies, which they must molt in order to grow.

Fiddler crabs, like lobsters, shrimp, and other crabs, are grouped with a class of arthropods called the Crustacea. Many have a shell-like carapace covering the **thorax**, or front part of the body. They also have two pairs of antennae. In the case of fiddler crabs, these antennae are short, and you may overlook them at first. Most crustaceans breathe through gills, and have a larval stage that looks quite different from the adults.

Long eyes, and a little lopsided

Female fiddlers have two front claws that are the same size. A male fiddler crab has one small front claw, and another extremely large one. When courting, he waves the large claw around in an attempt to attract a mate. He also uses it to warn other males away from the territory around his burrow. These waving motions remind some people of a violinist using a bow, therefore the name "fiddler crab" became this crab's common name.

A fiddler crab has two **compound eyes** at the end of little moving stalks called **peduncles**. The surface of each eye is quite rounded, giving the crab a very wide field of view. Crabs are able to see images, as well as sense light and dark, but they probably see a fuzzier, less distinct picture than we do.

43

Taxonomy

PHYLUM:
   Arthropoda (animals with paired, jointed legs and a hard exoskeleton)
CLASS: *Crustacea*
SUBCLASS: *Malacostraca*
SERIES: *Eumalacostraca*
SUPERORDER: *Eucarida*
ORDER: *Decapoda (8500 species of shrimp, lobsters, crayfish, and crabs)*
FAMILY: *Ocypododae (fiddler and ghost crabs)*
GENUS: *Uca (fiddler crabs)*
SPECIES: *Uca pugilator (sand fiddler), U. pugnax (mud fiddler), U. minax (brackish water fiddler), U. crenulata (California fiddler)*

Crayfish

Crayfish look like little lobsters. Both are decapods, or ten-legged crustaceans. They belong to different families, however, and live in different habitats. Lobsters are found in the ocean, but crayfish are freshwater animals. They are common in rivers, lakes, ponds, and streams. Some species climb about on land at night, returning to burrows in damp soil when they are through foraging for food.

Sensing danger, this crayfish prepares to defend itself.

On guard!

When you approach a crayfish, it may rear up its body and open its claws. This is a defensive posture many crayfish assume when they sense a threat. Crayfish have other postures and behaviors, too. If several are put in the same container, one may dominate the others, displaying aggressive behavior until the others retreat. Some may show a preference for certain places in the tank, or have a particular response to light or food. Crayfish behavior is interesting to study, and since many species are easy to care for, you can learn more about them at home.

Taxonomy

PHYLUM:
   Arthropoda (animals with paired, jointed legs and a hard exoskeleton)
CLASS: *Crustacea*
ORDER: *Decapoda*
FAMILY: *Astacidae, Cambarinae (some 500 species worldwide)*

Rearing crayfish

You can collect your own crayfish from a pond or lake, or order a few from a supply company (see p. 62). Keep them in an aquarium or plastic tub with a layer of clean gravel on the bottom. Some species do best in very shallow water (not quite covering their bodies) with plenty of surface area for oxygen exchange. Others will need deep water with a filter and aerator. If you collect your own, keep in mind that most crayfish do best in clean, well oxygenated water. Change the water daily if you are not filtering it; tap water is usually acceptable.

Both crayfish and goldfish live in this tub. During the day, the crayfish burrow in the mud around plant roots.

Put a few rocks in the tank so the crayfish can climb out of the water from time to time. Piled up rocks or clean clay flowerpots provide places for the crayfish to hide. If the tank is large with several hiding places, a few crayfish can be kept together. If you notice fighting or other aggressive behavior, they need more space.

Crayfish are scavengers, and will eat all sorts of food. You can offer them bits of raw meat, dog or cat food, and aquatic plants. Put the food right in front of them. If they don't start eating it within five minutes or so, remove it and try again later. Three feedings a week are adequate. Change the water after each feeding. Try feeding your crayfish in a small glass dish so it's easier to keep the tank water clean.

SPIDERS

Spiders belong to a class of arthropods called the arachnids. They have eight jointed legs and two body parts, the head (called the **cephalothorax** by scientists) and the **abdomen**. Spiders are carnivores; they eat other animals. Different species have different ways of hunting, but all eat in a similar fashion. Instead of biting and chewing food, spiders use their fangs to inject special digestive juices into their prey. These juices turn the prey's insides to liquid, which spiders then suck in through their mouths and swallow.

Making silk

All spiders produce silk in special glands inside their abdomens. The silk starts out as a liquid, but it hardens when it comes out of the tiny **spinnerettes** at the end of the abdomen. Spiders use little claws on their legs to direct the silk and to hold onto their webs.

Not all silk is the same. Some spiders make as many as six or seven different kinds of silk, each suited to a different purpose. A spider may use silk to make a web, wrap up prey, or spin a case for her eggs. Some spiders use scented silk to attract a mate, and others trail a line of silk behind them wherever they go.

Are spiders dangerous?

When you think of a spider, you may think of haunted houses, dark corners, and other places that give you the creeps. Spiders make lots of people nervous. Many people are afraid spiders will bite them, so they run from spiders, vacuum them up, or step on any they see.

For the most part, there is little reason to fear spiders. Spiders don't usually bite people who observe them without disturbing them. All spiders have poison glands that can paralyze insects and other small prey, but only a few produce poisons that are dangerous to humans. People vary in their sensitivity to spider bites, just as we vary in our sensitivity to poison ivy and bee venom.

One person might have an allergic reaction to a spider bite that would not affect another, so be careful when handling any spider. If you want to catch a spider so you can observe it more closely, gently scoop it up with a paper cup or plastic container.

Black widow females sometimes bite people and, though the bite itself doesn't hurt, the venom can make a person quite sick for several days. A bite from *Loxosceles laeta*, found in parts of South America, or the brown recluse (*Loxosceles reclusa*) of the United States, can cause serious illness and tissue damage. It's a good idea to find out if there are any potentially dangerous spiders in your area, and to learn to recognize them.

Finding spiders

Most buildings have resident spiders. Just look around your room! Corners that don't get vacuumed too frequently are good places to check. You will find some spiders on or near webs, and others roaming around walls or ceilings. Outdoors, just about any place is potential spider territory. Spiders live in mailboxes and cars, in weeds and in bushes. You can find them on neatly mowed lawns, walking across water, and in tunnels underground.

More about Spiders

 here are many kinds of spider webs. Some spiders weave webs that look like tiny mats on bark or fallen leaves. Others weave webs like "cobwebs" found in houses. Still others make funnels in stone walls and vegetation.

Orb-weavers

Some spiders make webs that have **radii** fanning out from a central **hub**. More strands are attached to the radii, and spiral around the hub. These webs are called **orb webs**. Many orb-weavers catch food in their webs during the day, but some catch moths, mosquitoes, and other insects that are active at night. A nighttime hunter often tears down its web in the morning and makes a new one in the evening. Though orb-weavers can repair damaged webs, most rebuild them daily. Spiders can "recycle" damaged webs by eating the silk.

Orb-weavers don't see very well, but they know they have caught something when their webs begin to vibrate. Insects struggling to free themselves cause the vibrations.

Garden spiders

You can recognize the garden spider, *Argiope aurantia*, by its beautifully patterned legs and body, and by the characteristic zigzag pattern, or **stabilimenta**, woven in the center of its web. There are many *Argiopes* in the world. All are large and hang head down in the center of their webs. Most build a web with a stabilimenta. Scientists aren't sure what the stabilimenta is for.

When the weather turns cold, garden spiders mate. A mated female will lay a mass of eggs and surround them with a special case spun from silk. The finished egg case is a half inch or so in diameter, and dangles from a plant stem. You might think the eggs inside would be best off waiting out the winter and hatching in the spring, but the eggs of *Argiope* and many other species hatch in the fall. The hatchling spiders do not leave the egg case, however; they stay inside until spring. Like adult spiders, they eat other small animals. The only small animals that happen to be inside the egg case are other tiny spiders, so *Argiope* hatchlings eat their siblings.

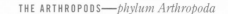
When spring arrives, whoever is left leaves the egg case and goes off to find a suitable place to build a web.

It is fascinating to open an egg case and observe the development of the baby spiders inside. Keep them in a jar or other container, and add some dampened sphagnum moss or a bit of sponge to humidify the air. Only collect an egg case if you can find others like it. That way, you will leave some spiders to develop in the usual fashion and populate your yard with another generation in the spring.

Some orb-weavers, like this spider in the genus Tetragnathas, *live in wetlands.*

Jumping spiders

Jumping spiders don't net insects in a web. They prowl around and pounce on prey instead. Their short, sturdy legs help them crawl quickly over the ground or up walls. Though they don't make webs, they do spin silk. Jumping spiders use silk to attach themselves to the surface they are crawling on before they pounce. If they miss their target, they climb back up the silk to where they started from. Some jumping spiders weave silk "cocoons" to spend the night in. Females surround their eggs with silk.

Jumping spiders have two large eyes and six smaller ones, which give them excellent vision. They are active during the day. Jumping spiders belong to the family Salticidae.

Keeping spiders

Ground-dwelling spiders can be kept in terraria or jars with sand or soil on the bottom, and a screen or cheesecloth lid on the top. Burrowing spiders need enough soil to tunnel into. Web-makers can be put in an empty aquarium or a large box with a glass or plastic side. Put a few sticks in your container for the spider to anchor its web to, but avoid filling it with soil or plants, which can become moldy. Feed captive spiders insects, and provide moisture with a piece of damp sponge or sphagnum moss. Gather your own sphagnum moss in a boggy area, or check to see if your local florist sells it.

Your big chance

Scientists have just begun to know and name the many different spiders on our planet. So far, about thirty thousand species have been described, but scientists continually collect spiders that can't be identified as one of these known species. There are probably over one hundred thousand species of spiders in the world, so if you want the chance to discover a new animal, study spiders!

49

Taxonomy

PHYLUM:
 Arthropoda (animals with paired, jointed legs and a hard exoskeleton)
SUBPHYLUM: *Chelicerata*
CLASS: *Arachnida (arthropods with four pairs of jointed legs and two body parts)*
ORDER: *Araneidae*
SUBORDER: *Labidognatha (true spiders, jaws are attached below the head and open sideways)*
GENUS: *Argiope*
SPECIES: *Argiope aurantia (black and yellow garden spider)*

Insects

 nsects are arthropods with six jointed legs and three main body parts. About three quarters of all known animal species are insects. Butterflies, beetles, flies, bugs, ants, and cockroaches are insects. Many of these animals are easy to find and fascinating to study.

This woodroach and this potato beetle are different species of insects. Like all other insects, they have six jointed legs, three main body parts, and they molt in order to grow.

Watching insects grow

Instead of growing gradually and continually larger, insects and other arthropods develop through a series of molts. Before molting, a new skin, or exoskeleton, forms underneath an insect's old one. During a molt, the old skin splits and the insect crawls out of it. The new skin is soft and stretchy at first. The insect's body and exoskeleton expand, then the new exoskeleton hardens. The insect will remain this new, slightly larger size until it molts again.

Some young insects look very much like their parents. They get larger with each molt, but otherwise they change relatively little. Other insects change dramatically as they grow, passing through stages that look completely different from one another. Watch crickets over a period of time to observe their growth, or **metamorphosis**, for yourself.

Crickets— from egg to nymph

 Crickets lay their eggs in the ground, so you aren't apt to see them! But you can find the tiny **nymphs** in the spring and early summer. Meadows, fields, gardens, and vacant lots are good places to find field crickets. There are different species of field crickets, all members of the genus *Gryllus*.

Newly hatched crickets look almost like tiny adults. They have long hind legs for jumping, two long antennae on their heads, and two tail-like **cerci** at the end of their abdomens. They don't look entirely like adults, though, because they don't have wings. On their backs are two small pads, which will develop into wings.

Becoming an adult

With each molt, a cricket's wing pads get larger and larger. Eventually, they become fully developed wings. Even fully grown, cricket wings are short, and adults are unable to fly. Male crickets use their wings to make sounds. By rubbing the edge of one wing against the other, males chirp to attract females, or to warn away intruders.

As female crickets grow, their wing pads grow, and they also develop a third tail-like projection between their two cerci. This is called the **ovipositor**, and it is used to lay eggs. A female cricket can push the end of the ovipositor into the ground and deposit her eggs through it. Though female crickets have wings, most females are silent.

Raising crickets

Catch a few crickets, and bring them home to study. House crickets (*Achaeta domesticus*) and field crickets are common in many areas. If you have trouble finding crickets, you can order them from a supply house (see p. 62). Some pet stores and bait shops also sell crickets.

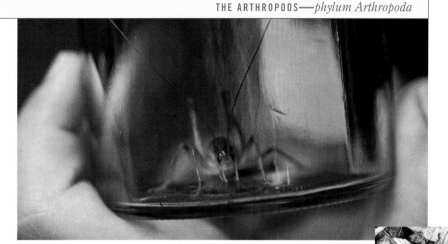

Keep crickets in a clear glass or plastic container so they will be easy to observe. Make sure your container has a tight fitting, screened lid. Layer an inch or two of sterilized sand or soil on the bottom. You can sterilize sand or soil by baking it in the oven for two hours at 200 degrees F. Add a few stones, cardboard tubes, or other hiding places. Mist the soil with water periodically. Keeping it slightly damp may encourage the females to lay eggs, but if it's too wet the eggs won't hatch.

Feed crickets dry dog food pellets and slices of fresh fruit or vegetables. Make sure to remove fresh food before it spoils. Crickets can get water from eating moist food, or from droplets of water sprinkled on the rocks in their cage. A small bottle of water plugged with a clean piece of sponge will also do.

Taxonomy

PHYLUM:
   Arthropoda (animals with paired, jointed legs and a hard exoskeleton)
CLASS: *Insecta*
ORDER: *Orthoptera (crickets, grasshoppers, and their relatives)*
FAMILY: *Gryllidae (crickets)*
GENERA: *Gryllus, Achaeta, and others*

Many crickets are **territorial**. If your container is small (a gallon fish tank or smaller) keep just one male and a female or two. Larger tanks can hold more, but overcrowding will lead to aggression and injury.

51

LEARNING FROM

Horseshoe crabs have been around a long time. For 250 million years or more, they've been crawling and swimming in the ocean. The ocean has changed during those years; continents have drifted, and new kinds of animals have evolved. Horseshoe crabs, however, have changed very little. *Limulus polyphemus,* the Atlantic horseshoe crab, looks remarkably like fossils of the *Limulus* species that lived during the age of dinosaurs. Though called the horseshoe crab, *L. polyphemus* is more closely related to spiders and scorpions than it is to other crabs. It belongs to the Merostomata, a class of arthropods that contains mostly extinct species known only from fossils. Horseshoe crabs are hardy animals, well adapted for life in the ocean and under no pressure to change.

Where to find horseshoe crabs

Limulus polyphemus can be found along the east coast of the United States. Other species of horseshoe crabs are found in China, Japan, and the East Indies. In the winter, Atlantic horseshoe crabs stay offshore, partly buried in bottom sediments. In May, start looking for them along the beach.

Horseshoe crabs mate in shallow water in the spring, and females lay eggs in the sand. Crabs of all sizes spend the summer near shore, heading back to deep water when the days get shorter.

How many eyes?!

Horseshoe crabs have two different kinds of eyes. Their large compound eyes can actually see images, as our eyes can. Smaller simple eyes tell light from dark. If you look at a horseshoe crab head-on, you'll notice one compound lateral eye on each side of its carapace, or shell, and a pair of simple eyes between them in the middle. The other simple eyes are difficult to make out. There is one beneath each lateral eye, another beneath the pair in the middle, two more on the crab's underside, and at least one on its spiky tail. Scientists know *Limulus* has an eye on its tail, even though they don't know exactly where it is. When they cover all its other eyes but leave the tail exposed, *Limulus* can still tell light from dark.

HORSESHOE CRABS

There are about 1,000 ommatidia, or simple eyes, in each compound eye. Each ommatidium contains a lens, 8-12 photoreceptors (light-sensitive cells), and a cell that sends information from the eye to the brain.

Shape and size may help horseshoe crabs recognize each other. Contrast, or how light or dark an object appears in relation to its background, may also be important. A male horseshoe crab will momentarily approach an object he can see, but if satisfied the object is not a female, he'll move on without attempting to mate. Heather Nelson is analyzing video tapes of horseshoe crabs in shallow water. By observing the approaches of real crabs to "dummies" painted different shades of black and grey, she can tell which of the "dummies" they see best.

Studying vision

Researchers have been studying the eyes of horseshoe crabs for more than fifty years. They have found that they contain some of the biggest light receptors in the animal kingdom. It's easier to observe large light receptors than tiny ones, so scientists who want to understand vision find that horseshoe crabs make good research animals. Horseshoe crabs are adaptable, too, able to live in a laboratory, away from their natural habitat. In the lab, scientists have recorded the signals that travel along nerve fibers from a crab's eye to its brain. They've figured out how the lenses, light receptors, and other parts of the eye function. These discoveries have led to a better understanding of human as well as horseshoe crab vision.

Scientists are also trying to understand what role vision plays in horseshoe crab behavior. Adult horseshoe crabs don't have predators to watch out for, and they don't need to see to find food; they encounter all sorts of edible plant and animal material as they crawl over the ocean floor. Bob Barlow and his colleagues suspected vision might play a role in mating. They tested their idea by putting "dummy" female crabs made of cement in shallow water, and watched the behavior of males that swam by. Sure enough, when male crabs swam close enough to notice the cement females, they turned towards, approached, and tried to mate with them. Males that were "blindfolded" with patches covering their eyes did not approach the cement females.

Taxonomy

PHYLUM:
  Arthropoda (animals with paired, jointed legs and a hard exoskeleton)
CLASS: Merostomata
ORDER: Xiphosura
FAMILY: Limulidae
GENUS: Limulus
SPECIES: L. polyphemus (Atlantic horseshoe crab)

Microinvertebrates

Some invertebrates are so small that you need a hand lens or microscope to see them. Viewed closely enough, tree bark, pond scum, drying mud, and human skin reveal hidden layers of life on earth. Exploring the tiny worlds that exist within the one we know is fascinating. Look carefully; you'll find that tiny invertebrates are everywhere!

Collecting for the microscope

There are countless places to look for microinvertebrates. Think small!

You can begin your exploration of the unseen with a pond study. Stagnant, green water, mud from along the shore, and the slimy coating on rocks and aquatic plants are all worth collecting. Plastic containers can be used to dig up mud, floating algae, and duckweed. Leaves and stems of rooted aquatic plants can also be collected. You can simply scoop up water in a jar, or drag a fine mesh plankton net through the water to concentrate your sample.

Observing your samples

Back home, get your samples ready to observe. Mud can be scraped into a plastic or enamel pan, and a little water poured over it. Aquatic plants can also be floated in pans of water. Jars containing water samples can be allowed to settle; leave the lids open a bit to allow fresh air to circulate.

Examine your samples with a hand lens to find tiny insect larvae, crustaceans, and molluscs that you might not have noticed when you were collecting. You may also find their eggs attached to plants, or floating in the water. A tiny leaf, drop of water, or bit of "slime" can be put on a glass slide under a compound microscope for an even closer look. Many of the animals you find may be unfamiliar and difficult to identify at first. Make drawings of the creatures you discover to help you recognize them when you see them again.

1 **2** **3**

4 **5** **6**

Buying magnifying equipment

There are many kinds of magnifiers. The cheapest and simplest to use is a hand lens. High quality plastic or glass hand lenses are available. Depending on the lens, these tools will allow you to magnify a specimen anywhere from three to ten times.

Another inexpensive and easy-to-use tool is the pocket microscope. Some have a battery-powered light, and can magnify as much as thirty times. Pocket microscopes are small and sturdy, so you can use them in the field as well as indoors. They cost between six and twenty dollars.

Compound microscopes are useful if you want to see very tiny animals. Specimens must be small enough to fit on a glass microscope slide, and thin enough for light to pass through them. Compound microscopes can magnify hundreds (sometimes even thousands) of times, making it possible to see things as small as individual cells. Compound microscopes vary widely in price. Sometimes high school and university science departments sell good, used microscopes for low prices when they are upgrading their equipment.

Dissecting microscopes, also called stereo microscopes, allow you to magnify large or opaque objects. They are great for examining pond animals, tree bark, insects, and soil. Because they have two eyepieces, these microscopes provide good depth of field, making it possible to get quite a bit of an object in focus at once. Unfortunately, even inexpensive dissecting scopes are several hundred dollars. Check to see if a local school or science center has one you can use.

Starfish

Starfish belong to the phylum Echinodermata. All echinoderms are marine animals, and all have bodies with five similar parts that surround a central axis. This kind of body organization is called **radial symmetry**. Our bodies show **bilateral symmetry**; our left side is basically a mirror image of our right.

Starfish anatomy

Most starfish have five arms, but some species may have as many as forty. If you find a starfish, gently pick it up and turn it over so you can see its underside, or **oral surface**. In the center of its body you will find the mouth. Rows of tube feet run along each arm. Most echinoderms have a hard, internal skeleton, sometimes with spines or bumps sticking out of it. The "top" side, or **aboral surface**, has a round bump called the **madreporite**. This bump is part of the system that circulates water within the starfish's body and works like a hydraulic system to operate the tube feet. Many echinoderms

use their tube feet to help them move around. Wastes are eliminated through an opening on the aboral surface, right in the center of the body. This opening is tiny, and may not be noticeable.

Strange table manners

When we eat a clam or mussel, we open the shell and take out the "meat." We put it in our mouths, chew, and swallow. It travels down a tube called the esophagus and enters our stomachs. There it stays, while acidic juices digest it.

Some starfish, like those in the genus *Asterias*, go about the whole thing differently. When one of these starfish finds a clam or mussel, it wraps its strong arms around the

shell. Hundreds of tiny tube feet on the bottom of each arm grab the shell like suction cups. The starfish pulls, and the shell opens a little. Then, by contracting the muscles of its body, the starfish pushes one of its two stomachs right out of its mouth and into the shell of its prey. The inside-out stomach starts digesting the prey by turning it into a thick liquid and absorbing it. A starfish may take hours to finish one clam or mussel, just as we take hours to digest the food we have swallowed.

Some starfish **evert** their stomachs and digest decaying plants or animals on the ocean floor. Some keep their stomachs inside and swallow prey whole. Others feed on tiny particles of food that get stuck to their bodies as they travel through mud and water.

Regeneration

If a starfish loses part of an arm, that part will grow back, or be regenerated. If an arm is lost along with part of the body, both the lost

arm and the rest of the starfish will regenerate, and two starfish will result. This is one way that starfish reproduce. Another way is by females releasing eggs into the water while males release sperm. Eggs that are fertilized hatch into tiny larvae, which eventually develop into starfish.

Regeneration is slow. It may take a year before an injured starfish has completely regrown a lost part.

Taxonomy

PHYLUM:
 Echinodermata (spiny-skinned marine animals)
CLASS: ***Stelleroidea (star-shaped, free-moving echinoderms with arms radiating out from a central disc)***
SUBCLASS: ***Asteroidea (starfish)***
ORDER: ***Forcipulatida***
GENUS: ***Asterias***
SPECIES: ***Asterias vulgaris (northern sea star)***

57

Echinoderms

Starfish aren't the only echinoderms. Their relatives live on rocky shores, sandy shores, and in the deep ocean.

Brittle stars

Brittle stars are common in the deep sea and in some shallow areas with soft bottoms. Like starfish, they have arms, but their arms are more flexible and more distinct from the round **central disc**. Brittle stars have tube feet, but they aren't used often for moving. Instead, brittle stars use one arm on each side like an oar, "rowing" themselves across the bottom of the ocean in awkward leaps and bounds.

If you look at the underside, or oral surface, of a brittle star, you'll see five triangular jaws with tooth-like projections. Some species use these jaws to scrape up **detritus**, or bottom muck containing bits of rotting plants and animals. Other brittle stars prey on small animals, or scavenge for dead ones. The arms and tube feet can help move food close to the jaws. Some brittle stars collect tiny particles of food by waving their mucus-covered arms about in the water.

Brittle stars, as well as starfish, are in the class Stelleroidea, but they form a separate subclass, the Ophiuroidea. Ophiuroids have just one stomach that they keep inside when they eat.

Sea urchins

Sea urchins are prickly animals. Their spherical bodies are covered with spines. It's not surprising that the class of echinoderms they belong to is named Echinoidea, which means "like a hedgehog." Sea urchins can move their spines by contracting small muscles at their base. Urchins can crawl around by moving their spines

Some gulls will drop an urchin on the ground to break it open.

and tube feet. The spines also offer protection. Though some predators, like gulls and sea otters, have found ways to get past the prickers, many animals avoid urchins. Some species of sea urchin even have chemicals in their spines that are irritating or toxic to animals that bite them, or people that accidentally step on them.

If you turn a sea urchin over, you will see its five teeth. Urchins use their teeth to graze on seaweed or gnaw on dead or unmoving animals. The teeth are part of a special chewing device called **Aristotle's lantern**. Only the teeth are visible on a live urchin, but if you find a **test**, or urchin skeleton, on the beach, look to see if the lantern is still intact.

Sand dollars

Sand dollars are found in parts of the ocean where the bottom is soft. They spend most of their time buried in one place. They eat the tiny particles of organic matter that are mixed in with the sand that covers them. Like sea urchins, they belong to the class Echinoidea, and are covered with spines. Their spines are quite short, though, and except for burrowing, sand dollars don't move much. Their round, flat skeletons, or tests, are often found by beachcombers.

Sea cucumbers

Sea cucumbers are soft-bodied echinoderms. Instead of a full skeleton, they have microscopic bony cells scattered throughout their body walls. That's why you won't find sea cucumber tests washed up on the beach! Sea cucumbers are **sedentary** animals that lie under rocks or burrow into the sand. They filter plankton and organic matter out of the water with sets of elaborately branching tentacles. To eat, a sea cucumber stuffs a tentacle into its "mouth," then slowly pulls it back out, scraping off food particles as it goes.

Sea cucumbers, like other echinoderms, are able to regenerate some parts of their bodies. Some species can regenerate one end of the body if it is lost or damaged. Others can regenerate their internal organs. Strangely, sea cucumbers sometimes **eviscerate**, or eject their internal organs into the water! Scientists aren't sure why this unusual behavior occurs.

There are about five hundred different sea cucumber species. Together, they make up the order Holothuroidea.

The hairy cucumber at the left, Sclerodactyla briareus, *has pulled all of its tentacles into its body. This often happens when the animal is disturbed. You can see the hundreds of tiny tube feet that cover its body. Some holothuroideans lack tube feet.*

Taxonomy

PHYLUM:
    Echinodermata (spiny-skinned marine animals)
CLASSES: *Stelleroidea (starfish and brittle stars), Echinoidea (sea urchins and sand dollars), Holothuroidea (sea cucumbers)*
ORDERS: *Arbacioda, Echinoida, and others*
GENERA: *Arbacia, Strongylocentrotus, and others*
SPECIES: *Arbacia punctulata (Atlantic purple sea urchin), Strongylocentrotus droebachiensis (green sea urchin)*

The Chordates

The phylum Chordata is a large, diverse group of animals. It includes three subphyla. One is the vertebrates, or animals with backbones. Mammals (including humans), birds, reptiles, amphibians, and fish make up this group. The other two groups are invertebrate chordates, including the Urochordata, or tunicates.

Tunicates

Tunicates are marine animals with a test or **tunic**, covering their bodies. This tunic is partly made of cellulose, a sugar ordinarily found in the cell walls of plants, but unusual in the bodies of animals. A siphon, or tube, pulls seawater into a tunicate's body, where a special chamber filters out the microscopic organisms it feeds on. Another siphon squirts out filtered water. If you disturb a tunicate, it may shoot water out of both siphons at once, so tunicates are commonly called "sea squirts." The sea vase and sea peach are different kinds of tunicates.

Many tunicates start out as free-swimming larvae, then attach themselves to a rock, shell, or other object as they mature. The golden star tunicate, *Botryllus schlosseri*, forms a thin crust on rocks. It is actually not one animal, but a colony of many individuals. The individuals are clustered in star shaped groups, with a number of groups sharing one rubbery tunic. Each individual has one siphon of its own, which it uses to pull in seawater. Instead of a second siphon, the individuals in a cluster share a central opening to filter water out.

Distant cousins

During some phase of their lives, all chordates have gills, a dorsal nerve chord (one that runs along the back), and a notochord (a flexible rod that helps support the body).

relatives. Remember, we belong to the phylum Chordata just like they do. In fact, tunicates are more closely related to people than they are to any of the other animals in this book!

The phrase "during some phase of their lives" is important here, for many chordates "outgrow" a particular characteristic as they develop. People, for example, breathe through lungs, but we have gills when we are embryos. Adult tunicates don't have a dorsal nerve chord or a notochord; larvae have both, so scientists group them with the chordates. You may find sea squirts when you visit the seashore. When you do, consider them close

You might not think you have too much in common with a sea squirt, but in the early stages of development people and sea squirts share some physical characteristics.

Continuing

O nce you get interested in invertebrates, you'll find you notice them and think about them more and more. Explore a pond or seashore, your backyard, a schoolyard, or a city park for invertebrates—you'll notice interesting things and fascinating behavior you may once have overlooked. Visit a nature center, aquarium, or maritime center in your area; they often have exhibits and collections of living and preserved specimens you can look at, and sometimes touch.

It's amazing to realize that the different animals in this book represent just seven of the twenty-six phyla that contain invertebrates. You can continue your study of invertebrate zoology by learning about animals in a few new phyla. Or, you may already have discovered a particular species or group that fascinates you and be ready to specialize...

How to Order Specimens and Supplies

T he most enjoyable way to study invertebrates is to collect as many of the specimens as you can yourself. Depending on the season or where you live, it is sometimes difficult to collect live specimens. You'll be surprised at how easy it is to adapt everyday pans, bowls, and other kitchen and hobby supplies to fit your needs. But some equipment, such as microscopes, can't be adapted or built.

Almost all of the equipment and specimens mentioned in *Invertebrate Zoology* can be ordered through the mail or by phone from a company called Carolina Biological Supply. If you want to order by phone, you'll need an adult with a credit card. A handling charge is added to each order.

EASTERN U.S.
Carolina Biological Supply
2700 York Road
Burlington, NC 27215
Toll free 1-800-334-5551

WESTERN U.S.
Carolina Biological Supply
Box 187
Gladstone, OR 97027
Toll free 1-800-547-1733

Please remember: If you order live specimens, make sure you have everything you need to feed and house them before they arrive.

If you can't find *Earthworms* (pages 14-15), you can order 12 medium size specimens for about $7.00; a 12 ounce bag of "Magic Worm Food" will cost about $2.50. Three medium size pond *Leeches* (pages 16-17) cost about $7.50. Saltwater sponges (pages 20-23) are pretty expensive, but you can order a freshwater *Spongilla* Review Set, which includes a live sponge culture, a pad of Sponge Anatomy Bioreview Sheets, and instructions for about $13.00. A Micro-Pac of 12 glass *Microscope slides and cover glasses* for looking at sponges costs about $4.00, or you can order a Disposable Lab Pack of 50 plastic slides

and covers for about $11.00. You can order 12 brown *Planaria* (pages 24-27) for about $5.00. Carolina also sells a Planaria Heads and Tails Kit for studying regeneration. It comes with 25 planaria, 2 razor blades, petri dishes, water, and instructions for about $21.00. Carolina sells 12 *Land Snails* (pages 28-29) for about $8.50, but you can't order them in California without a special permit since they are considered pests. You can get clams (pages 32-33) for dissection from your local fish store, or a preserved Long-necked *Clam* from Carolina for about $2.00. Whole squid (pages 34-35) are also pretty easy to get from many fish stores, and Carolina sells a large plain *Squid* preserved in a "Caropak" for about $4.00. You can order 6 small to medium size *Crayfish* (pages 44-45) for about $10.00, but crayfish can't be shipped into California. It's not hard to capture crickets (pages 50-51) yourself, but you can order 12 live House *Cricket* Adults for about $6.00, or a "Little Chirper" Cricket Cage, which comes with a cage, six live crickets, and food for about $12.00. Microscopes (pages 54-55) can be very expensive. For field trips Carolina sells a Folding Pocket *Magnifier*, Single for about $4.50, which provides up to 5X magnification, Double for about $7.50, which provides up to 10X magnification. If you want to get more ambitious, you can order either a 10X Miniscope for about $24.00, or the Panasonic Light Scope which is a 30X portable microscope for about $35.00; both come with lights and batteries.

ATTENTION TEACHERS: *Most of the equipment and specimens are available at quantity discounts for classroom use. In addition to Carolina Biological Supply, these supplies are also available from Science Kit and Boreal Laboratories (1-800-828-7777) and Wards Natural Science Establishment (1-800-962-2660).*

Glossary

abdomen: the rear body section of an arthropod.

aboral surface: in echinoderms, the top side.

aerate: to expose to air, or bubble air into a liquid.

aestivate: to spend time in an unmoving state during a period of hot or dry weather.

anterior: near the front.

aquatic: living in water.

Aristotle's lantern: the chewing mouthparts of a sea urchin.

benchmark: the spot chosen to serve as the "zero point" on a transect line.

beneficial animal: any of various animals that are helpful to people. They eat our pests, or provide us with food and materials.

bilateral symmetry: similar halves divided by a midline.

bivalve: a mollusc with a two-part shell.

brood: to incubate eggs within the body.

buds: pieces of a sponge that break off and develop into new sponges.

carapace: in horseshoe crabs and crustaceans, the part of the exoskeleton that covers the head and thorax.

carnivore: an animal-eater.

castings: soil or sediment swallowed by a worm and excreted at the entrance of its tunnel or burrow.

caudal sucker: the sucker at the rear end of a leech's body that helps it to move.

central disc: the round, middle part of a brittle star's body.

cephalothorax: in spiders, the body part that includes the head.

cerci: abdominal appendages on some insects that pick up information about the surrounding environment.

chemoreceptors: cells that detect chemicals.

chromatophores: cells that contain pigment.

cilia: minute, moving, hair-like structures on some cells.

cirri: finger-like projections, sometimes used to filter food.

class: a group of living things. Each phylum is divided into classes, and each class is further divided into orders.

clitellum: the light-colored "collar" around the body of an earthworm.

commensal: an organism that lives in or on the body of another without causing it any harm.

compound eye: an eye made up of many simple eyes that function together.

decline: decreasing slope; downhill.

detritus: fragments of organic matter, such as bits of decaying plants and animals.

dioecious: having separate sexes.

domestic animal: any of various animals that are used and raised by people.

dormant: inactive; resting.

dorsal nerve chord: the nerve chord that runs along the back of animals in the phylum Chordata. In humans, the spinal chord.

epidermis: the outer layer of skin.

evert: to turn inside out.

eviscerate: to remove or eject the stomach.

exhalent siphon (also called the excurrent siphon): in some invertebrates, an opening or tube that carries water out of an animal's body.

exoskeleton: the hard, outside body covering of an arthropod.

family: a group of living things. Each order is divided into families, and each family is further divided into genera.

filter feeder: an animal that strains minute organisms or particles of food from water.

flagella: whip-like structures on some cells.

free-living: animals that do not live in or on the bodies of other animals; not a parasite.

gemmules: cells that produce new individuals of their own species.

genus (genera [pl.]): a group of living things. Each family is divided into genera, and each genus is further divided into species.

gills: organs capable of extracting oxygen from water.

gonads: reproductive glands; testes or ovaries.

gonopore: in some female molluscs, the opening that receives the male penis.

habitat: an organism's environment.

herbivore: a plant-eater.

hermaphrodite: an animal that has both male and female reproductive organs.

hirudin: a chemical in a leech's saliva that keeps its host's blood from clotting.

homogeneous: having similar anatomy, and the same ancestry.

host: an organism with one or more parasites living in or on it.

hub: the central portion of some spider webs.

incline: increasing slope; uphill.

infauna: animals that burrow in soft bottom sediments.

inhalent siphon (also called the incurrent siphon): in some invertebrates, an opening or tube that pulls water into an animal's body.

ink sac: in squid, the organ that contains the inky, protective secretions.

invertebrate: an animal without a backbone.

isolate: to remove.

lateral eye: eyes located on the side of a horseshoe crab's carapace.

madreporite: in echinoderms, the place on the body surface where water can be taken in or let out.

mantle: a layer of tissue unique to molluscs.

mantle cavity: in molluscs, the space underneath the mantle.

margin: the edge of a shell, or of one valve of a bivalve shell.

marine gastropod: any gastropod mollusc that lives in salt water.

metamorphosis: a physical change of form some animals undergo as they develop.

molt: to shed the exoskeleton, or skin.

mop: many strands of squid eggs deposited in the same place by many different females.

mucus: a moist, sticky, or slimy secretion.

notochord: a long, flexible rod that runs along the back of every animal in the phylum Chordata during some phase of its life.

nymphs: the young of insects with gradual metamorphosis.

oral sucker: the sucker at the front end of a leech's body that helps it to move.

oral surface: in echinoderms, the underside, or side with the mouth.

orb webs: spider webs characterized by radii fanning out from a central hub, with a spiral of silk connecting the radii.

order: a group of living things. Each class is divided into orders, and each order is further divided into families.

oscula: large pores through which filtered water leaves the body of a sponge.

osphradium: a chemically sensitive structure near the gills of some molluscs.

ovipositor: an anatomical feature used to deposit eggs.

parasite: an organism that lives in or on other organisms. Parasites typically weaken, and sometimes kill, their hosts.

peduncles: in some crabs, stalks that hold the eyes away from the carapace.

pen: the internal shell of a squid.

pest: a species that annoys people, or causes harm to food crops or property.

pharynx: part of the digestive tube of some animals, found between the mouth and the stomach.

photonegative: avoiding light.

photophores: cells that produce light.

phylum (phyla [pl.]): a group of animals, and the primary divisions in the animal kingdom.

proboscis: in invertebrates, a straw-like appendage that is extended to detect food or chemicals, or to feed.

radial symmetry: similar parts organized around a central axis.

radii: silk strands that fan out from the center of some spider webs.

radula: a file-like structure in a gastropod's mouth, used to scrape food.

reaggregation: reassembling parts to form a whole.

regeneration: the process of growing back tissues or structures that have been removed or destroyed. A method of reproduction in some animals.

scavenger: an organism that eats dead plants and animals, or garbage.

scuta and terga: in acorn barnacles, the two central pairs of plates that form a "door."

sedentary: permanently attached.

segmented body: an animal's body, made of a number of similar sections.

sessile: attached.

setae: bristle-like organs on some animals.

simple eyes: eyes capable of detecting light and dark.

siphon: an opening or tube used to bring water in or out of an animal's body.

species: divisions within a genus of distinct kinds of organisms. Members of the same species can mate and produce more organisms like themselves.

spicules: needle-like structures that form the "skeleton" of some sponges.

spinnerettes: in a spider, the organ that produces threads of silk from the secretions of silk glands.

stabilimenta: the zigzag pattern *Argiope* spiders weave into their webs.

survey: a detailed study.

tactile cells: cells that are sensitive to touch.

taxonomist: a scientist interested in classification.

tentacles: long, flexible appendages on many invertebrates, used as sensory organs or to grab food.

territorial: having to do with a given area or territory. A territorial insect may try to keep intruders away from a particular place.

test: the shed exoskeleton of a crab or horseshoe crab, or the skeleton of a sea urchin.

thorax: the front body section of an arthropod.

transect: a line that runs through a particular area.

transect site: the area where a transect is set up.

transverse fission: splitting apart crosswise rather than lengthwise.

tube feet: small, tube-like appendages on echinoderms that are used for feeding, moving, or as sensory organs.

tunic: the layer of tissue that covers a tunicate's body.

umbo: the oldest part of a bivalve mollusc's shell.

valve: one part of a two-part mollusc shell.

veliger larvae: the tiny, swimming young of some molluscs.

ventral: the "belly" side of an animal.

vents: openings on the surface of a sponge that push water out of the sponge's body.

vertebrate: an animal with a backbone.

wild animal: an animal that is neither tame nor raised by people.

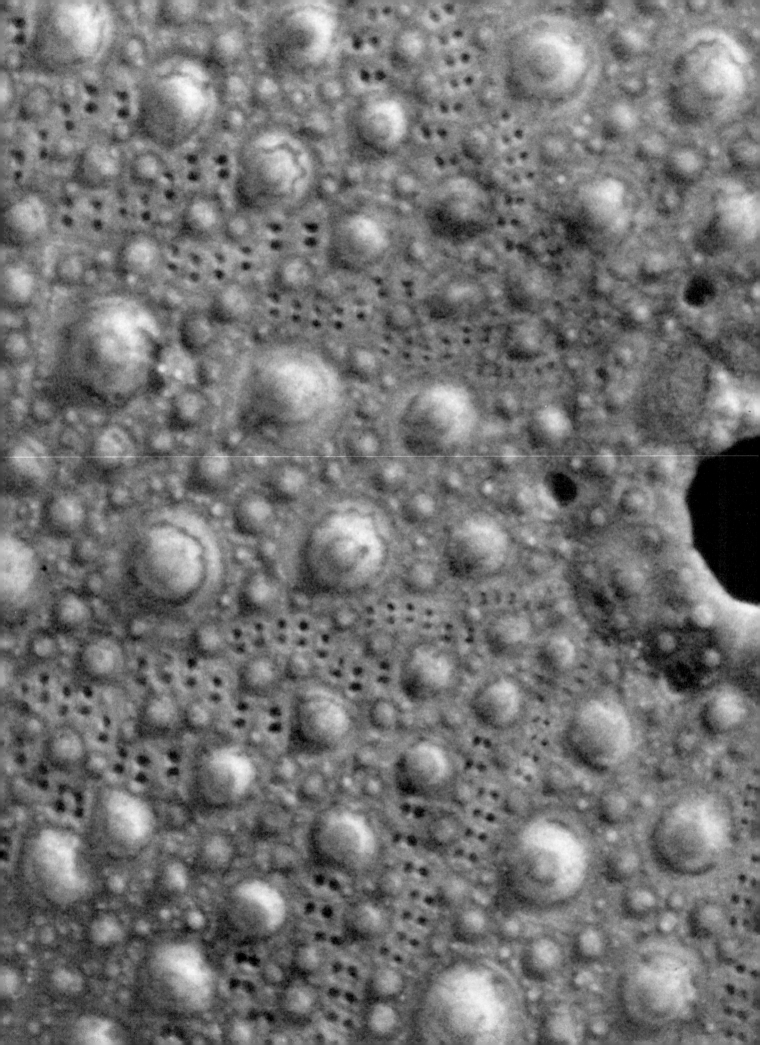